# NEW ORLEANS
## PIANO STYLES

A GUIDE TO THE
KEYBOARD LICKS OF
CRESCENT CITY GREATS

BY TODD LOWRY

HAL•LEONARD®

ISBN 978-1-4768-8690-9

Published by:
Hal Leonard Corporation
7777 W. Bluemound Rd.
P.O. Box 13819
Milwaukee, WI 53213

Printed in the U.S.A.

First Edition

Visit Hal Leonard Online at
**www.halleonard.com**

# Contents

# Introduction

New Orleans. The Crescent City. The Big Easy. The home of the eternal party. The city where funerals turn into street parades. City of rhythms. Good times rolling. Red beans cooking. Mardi Gras. The French Quarter. Bourbon Street.

There's no other place on earth quite like New Orleans — famous for its cuisine, Mardi Gras, and its music. A major U.S. port and the largest city in the state of Louisiana, it is known for its cross-cultural and multilingual heritage.

Founded in 1718 by the French, New Orleans was ceded to the Spanish Empire in 1763. It remained under Spanish control until 1801, when it reverted to French control. Napoleon then immediately sold the territory to the United States in the Louisiana Purchase of 1803.

The city grew rapidly with influences of French, Spanish, Creole, Irish, German, Native American, Cajun, and African ethnicities. This incredible mix of people and cultures has contributed to the unique fusion that is New Orleans music.

The city's attitude toward race differed from general practices in the U.S. during slavery. Africans were allowed to retain their own language, beliefs, and customs. In the early 19th century, slaves were allowed to congregate in the area known as Congo Square for dancing to the rhythms of their homelands on Sunday afternoons. New Orleans was the only North American city to allow this. Undoubtedly this led to both the preservation and the flowering of African music.

New Orleans celebrates Mardi Gras (Fat Tuesday) and uninhibited partying. New Orleans relishes dances and parades. Even funerals eventually turn into parades. The largest of the city's many music festivals is the New Orleans Jazz & Heritage Festival, which takes place every year in late April and early May.

With all due respect to Satchmo, the *piano* has been the most important instrument in the development of New Orleans music. Professor Longhair, James Booker, Dr. John, Allen Toussaint, Harry Connick Jr., Fats Domino, Jelly Roll Morton — all piano players — they've been its prime innovators.

This book/CD is a guide to various styles and techniques used by the great New Orleans pianists. The pianists represent New Orleans piano from the earliest origins of jazz and blues to their modern form.

# The Recording

On the accompanying CD, you'll find demonstrations of all the musical examples in the book. Practice slowly at first, using a metronome to help you keep a steady beat. As you become more proficient, increase the metronome speed gradually over a period of days and weeks, until you reach the indicated metronome markings.

All tracks were recorded by Brent Edstrom.

# CHAPTER 1
# EARLY JAZZ STYLES

The abolition of slavery led to new opportunities for freed African-Americans. Although segregation limited employment opportunities for most blacks, many were able to find work in entertainment – in dances, minstrel shows, and vaudeville. Black pianists played in bars, clubs, and brothels.

In 1897, prostitution was officially legalized in a part of New Orleans known as Storyville.

For the next 20 years, Storyville became a haven for adult entertainment, including dancing, alcohol consumption, and a new style of improvisational music called "jazz." New Orleans is generally regarded as the birthplace of jazz, and New Orleans jazz ultimately became the foundation of jazz itself. Early New Orleans jazz is commonly referred to as "Dixieland jazz."

The great players of early New Orleans jazz include cornetist Buddy Bolden, trumpeter Louis Armstrong, the Original Dixieland Jazz Band, and pianist Jelly Roll Morton. Some of the standards they played are "When the Saints Go Marching In," "Basin Street Blues," "Muskrat Ramble," "Tiger Rag," and "Tin Roof Blues."

The sporting houses in Storyville usually employed a solo piano player to entertain guests. Those with extensive repertoires became known as "professors." **Jelly Roll Morton** (1890–1941; born Ferdinand Joseph LaMothe) was one of those "professors."

One of the most colorful characters in American music, Morton worked as a bordello pianist, pimp, pool shark, gambler, and comedian before establishing himself as a musician and recording artist. He took his nickname from his 1915 composition "Jelly Roll Blues," which was published as the first jazz arrangement in print. He was also an insufferable braggart. He once claimed to have invented jazz in the year 1902 (when he was 12 years old).

Despite this dubious claim, Morton was legitimately one of the first true jazz composers and one of the most important figures in early jazz. He represents the common roots and the link between ragtime, jazz, and stride. His music is still played today.

Morton's piano style developed partly from ragtime. Like ragtime, it features an "oom-pah" bass, i.e., an alternating bass note and medium range chord.

TRACK 1

*Figure 1 – Ragtime bass*

Ragtime, however, was played with straight eighth notes. Morton loosened ragtime's rhythmic stiffness in favor of swung notes. That is, the second of each pair of eighth notes was played on the last third of the beat rather than on the midpoint between beats. The underlying triplet feel is central to what we call "swing" or a "shuffle."

Morton considered the Cuban tresillo/habanera rhythm, which he called the "Spanish Tinge," to be an essential ingredient of jazz. This rhythm can be heard in his left hand on his song "New Orleans Blues."

TRACK 2

*Figure 2 – "The Spanish Tinge"*

Morton composed "The Pearls" as a valentine to a Kansas City waitress. This version is from his Library of Congress recordings, made late in his life in 1938. The song is marked by the harmonically adventurous use of the ♭VI7 chord (E♭7 in the key of G). "The Pearls" incorporates the "oom-pah" bass, occasional melodic lines in the bass (bars 3 and 9), and parallel tenth triads (bar 18).

The right-hand melody is thickened with octaves and occasional chords spanning less than an octave. The arrangement is similar to stride styles.

Morton uses grace notes in bars 19 and 20. A grace note is a quick ornamental tone played directly before a main note. The notes are connected in music notation with a slur marking. These grace notes are similar to "bending" a note, like a guitar player might bend a string. Obviously, each note on the piano is a discrete pitch so we can't actually bend a note. However, we can use grace notes as the closest approximation. These grace notes lead into the third of the key, B.

Also note the triplet figures in the left hand at bars 18-19. Professor Longhair, discussed later in this book, was fond of such melodic figures, which are similar to the "ruffs" of a drummer.

TRACK 3

*Figure 3 – "The Pearls"*

**The Pearls**
By Ferd "Jelly Roll" Morton

# CHAPTER 2
# STRIDE STYLES

Stride piano is a solo jazz piano style that developed in the 1920s and 1930s.

Stride adapted ragtime's left-hand pattern to form the distinctive stride bass. In its most basic form, the stride bass is an alternation of bass notes and mid-range chords.

*Figure 4 – Typical Stride Bass*

TRACK 4

Pianists sometimes used tenths in place of single bass notes. They also used walking tenths and walking tenths triads.

Stride is basically a virtuosic music, calling for fast tempos, full use of the piano's range, and a wide array of pianistic devices. Stride is still popular and it has influenced other styles.

**Isidore "Tuts" Washington** (1907–1984) exemplified the stride tradition. He was active musically from the 1920s to 1984. Born in New Orleans, Washington taught himself piano at age 10. He started out in brothels and honky-tonks.

He was a prototypical New Orleans pianist: he played blues but also learned rags and jazz because the city's tradition demanded a wide repertoire. He was already performing regularly when the stock market crashed in 1929. He did not record until 1984, when, at the age of 76, he finally recorded his first and only album. His final years were spent playing in the pleasant surroundings of luxury hotels.

Following is an arrangement of "When the Saints Go Marching In" in the style of Tuts Washington. The arrangement is played very quickly, in presto tempo.

1. There is a short introduction in bars 1-4.

2. The melody is thickened with octaves and occasional chords, usually spanning an octave.

3. The arrangement departs immediately from the typical stride bass pattern, with a full triad on beat one in bar 5.

4. There are walking tenths in the left hand at bars 11-12.

5. There are walking octaves in the left hand at bar 35.

6. Bar 37 features a four-bar break with only the right hand playing.

7. Bar 41 features a walking bass outlining triads, while the right hand improvises.

8. In bar 54, note the interesting chord substitution of Gbmaj7 (bII) for C7.

9. There's a "shout chorus" starting at bar 57 with the repetition of a two-beat melodic figure in bars 61–64.

TRACK 5

*Figure 5 – "When the Saints Go Marching In"*

**When the Saints Go Marching In**
Words by Katherine E. Purvis
Music by James M. Black

**James Carroll Booker III** (1939–1983) was classically trained, a child prodigy, and a virtuosic player whose performances combined elements of stride, blues, and classical styles. Booker was able to play anything from pop tunes to classical pieces to jazz standards. The songs on his recordings include Chopin's "Minute Waltz," "Eleanor Rigby," "King of the Road," "Malagueña," "Goodnight, Irene" and "He's Got the Whole World in His Hands."

Booker made his recording debut at age 15. As a young man he recorded "ghost" piano tracks for Fats Domino. Booker was called by his peers "the piano prince of New Orleans." But he was a man of bizarre eccentricities whose life was a study in struggle. In retrospect, he may have been mentally ill. At some point he lost his left eye. There are various stories about how this happened – a street fight, a prison brawl, or a dirty needle. He had severe problems with heroin and cocaine, exhibited erratic behavior, spent time in Angola Prison and died at the age of 43 in the emergency ward of Charity Hospital.

Booker's version of "On the Sunny Side of the Street" from his album "New Orleans Piano Wizard Live!" is typically virtuosic.

First, note Booker's stride pattern in his left hand. He consistently plays an octave, an octave plus another interval, or a tenth on beats 1 and 3. Then he anticipates the notes on beats 1 and 3 with partial chords on the preceding upbeats.

In the right hand he thickens the melody with octaves, block chords spanning an octave, and grace notes. Not only that, he elaborates on the melody. Figure 6 shows the song's composed melody and how Booker elaborates on it in the first eight bars. He continues in this manner throughout the piece.

*Figure 6 – Melodic comparison*

TRACK 6

There's no introduction. Booker simply plays through the first chorus of the song.

*Figure 7 – "On the Sunny Side of the Street," first chorus*

TRACK 7

Near the end of the song Booker enters with his vocals. He begins to play rolling octaves with his left hand, rocking the beat. The ending bit, starting at bar 15, is some campy fun.

TRACK 8

*Figure 8 – "On the Sunny Side of the Street," ending*

I'm talk - in' 'bout the sun - ny side, _ the sun - ny side, a - bout the

sun - ny un - ny un - ny side, _____ sun - ny side of the street.

# CHAPTER 3
# BLUES STYLES

Blues is both a musical form and a music genre that originated in African-American communities around the end of the 19th century. It developed from spirituals, work songs, field hollers, shouts, and chants. Jelly Roll Morton reported having heard blues for the first time In New Orleans in 1902.

The blues form, ubiquitous in jazz, R&B, and rock 'n' roll, is characterized by specific chord progressions of which the 12-bar blues chord progression is the most common. The form crystallized in the first decade of the 20th century. The 12-bar blues chord progression is repeated for both the melody and the improvised solo parts of the song.

*Figure 9 – The 12-bar blues form*

TRACK 9

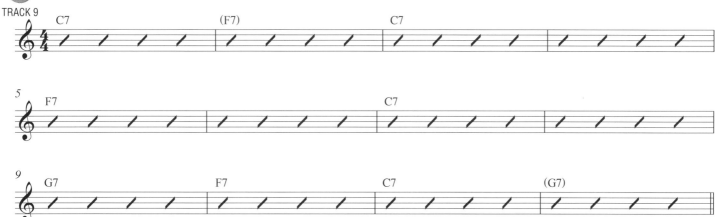

All the chords are dominant seventh chords built on the first, fourth, and fifth degrees of the key, which we refer to as the I7, IV7, and V7 chords. Bars 11 and 12 are a "turnaround" section leading back to the beginning of the form.

Other chord progressions, such as eight-bar forms, are also considered blues. The eight-bar blues is popular in New Orleans music.

*Figure 10 – The eight-bar blues form*

TRACK 10

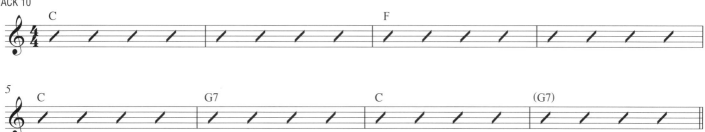

It's vital to develop a solid left-hand groove when playing the blues. The left hand propels the rhythm while defining the harmonic progressions. Figure 11 shows several possible left-hand patterns.

*Figure 11 – Left-hand blues patterns*

TRACK 11

An indispensable part of the New Orleans piano vocabulary is the crossover right-hand lick. Dr. John calls this "The Famous Lick." Following are several possible licks, all of which work over a C or C7 chord.

 *Figure 12 – "Famous Licks"*

TRACK 12

Measures 11 and 12 in the 12-bar blues progression present possibilities for blues turnarounds or endings.  Turnarounds lead to a V7 chord in preparation for going back to the top of the form. One basic turnaround is simply a descending bass line.

*Figure 13 – Bass line turnaround*

TRACK 13

When we add chords and motion, we've got several possible turnarounds.

*Figure 14 – Three Turnarounds*

TRACK 14

Endings lead back to the I7 or tonic chord. Here are two possible endings.

TRACK 15

*Figure 15 – Two Endings*

# BARRELHOUSE PIANO

In the late 1880s, in outlying areas of Louisiana, lumber and mining camps arose. With them came barrelhouses – taverns where beer was sold from big wooden barrels. Pianos, often castoffs, occupied the center of entertainment in these rundown honky-tonks. These were the beginnings of "barrelhouse" piano. Piano players in the barrelhouse didn't tickle the ivories; they smashed them. The trick was to make themselves heard and the best way to do that was to play and sing loud.

**William Thomas Dupree**, known as **Champion Jack Dupree**, was the embodiment of the New Orleans blues and boogie pianist, a barrelhouse "professor." Dupree's birth date is disputed: it's 1908, 1909, or 1910. He died in 1992. He was born in New Orleans but left as a young man to live the itinerant life of a musician.

He taught himself to play and apprenticed with Tuts Washington, but got most of his experience in barrelhouses and other drinking establishments. He met boxer Joe Louis, who encouraged him to become a boxer and he ultimately fought in 107 bouts.

The typical barrelhouse blues left-hand pattern consists of alternation between intervals of a fifth and a sixth.

*Figure 16 – Typical barrelhouse left hand*

TRACK 16

In 1940, Champion Jack Dupree made the first recording of "The Junker's Blues," an eight-bar blues. The left hand he played on the recording was even more primitive than the typical barrelhouse style. It was simply octaves and fifths played in an eighth-note shuffle rhythm. This song would play a significant role in New Orleans music history

*Figure 17 – Blues as played by Champion Jack Dupree*

TRACK 17

Next we have a blues in the style of "Crescent City Bounce" by **Archibald** (**Leon T. Gross**; 1916–1973). Archibald was one of the last barrelhouse pianists. Born in New Orleans, he was a working musician by the 1930s. He influenced Dr. John, Fats Domino, Huey "Piano" Smith, and James Booker, but he died leaving behind only 11 recorded tracks.

Figure 18 uses a standard left-hand pattern. The first chorus is based on a riff forming a ninth chord, which is repeated on each chord of the form. The second chorus includes some aggressive 16th notes.

*Figure 18 – Blues in the style of "Crescent City Bounce" by Archibald*

TRACK 18

Here's a blues in the style of "Honky Tonk" by Tuts Washington. The left-hand pattern is the same as in the previous example. The right hand is quite melodic. Note the use of thirds in bar 6 and the use of sixths in bars 9–10. Thirds are also used to good effect in bars 21–22. The ending on the parallel ninth chords is a bit of a spoof.

*Figure 19 Blues in the style of "Honky Tonk" by Tuts Washington*

The next example is a fast blues in the style of "Red Beans" by **Marcia Ball** (*b*1949), who grew up in Vinton, Louisiana and who was influenced by Professor Longhair. This piece is played with straight eighths. The left-hand part is a typical blues pattern. The right hand plays exclusively in G pentatonic, with grace notes common on the blue note of A♯.

*Figure 20 Blues in the style of "Red Beans" by Marcia Ball*

TRACK 20

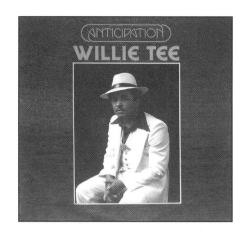

Figure 21 is a modern blues variation in the style of "In the Beginning" by **Willie Tee** (1944–2007), pianist, songwriter, and an early architect of New Orleans funk and soul. He uses substitute chords in bars 7–8 to give the blues a new twist.

TRACK 21

*Figure 21 – Blues in the style of "In the Beginning" by Willie Tee*

# CHAPTER 4
# BOOGIE WOOGIE STYLES

Boogie woogie is a style of piano-based blues that became popular in the 1930s after barrelhouse morphed into the newer style.

The essence of boogie woogie is its blues structure, fast pace, propulsive eight-to-the-bar left-hand figures outlining chords, and free-wheeling blues licks in the right hand. The style demands skillful hand independence. Boogie woogie is still very popular, as listeners respond positively to its excitement and propulsive rhythm.

Most boogie woogie tunes are 12-bar blues, but the style has been applied to popular songs, such as "Swanee River."

**Clarence "Pine Top" Smith** is generally credited with introducing the term "boogie woogie" into widespread use starting in 1929 when he recorded his "Pine Top's Boogie Woogie." Smith died tragically at age 24, victim of a random shooting in a club where he was performing.

There are countless left-hand patterns devised by the great boogie woogie pianists. Here are a few.

TRACK 22

*Figure 22 – Boogie Woogie bass figures*

A common technique in boogie woogie is the tremolo. A tremolo is the rapid oscillation between two distinct tones or combinations of tones.

TRACK 23

*Figure 23 – Tremolo*

Tremolos occur frequently on thirds, sixths, or octaves. Sometimes a tremolo consists of a whole chord. Tremolos can be performed by both hands and can be combined with other ornamentations, such as grace notes.

The "Swanee River Boogie" is based on "Old Folks at Home" (aka "Way Down Upon the Swanee River") by Stephen Foster. Fats Domino recorded it under the title "Swanee River Hop." Dr. John has frequently performed it.  It's not a blues, but the harmony is all I-IV-V. The left-hand boogie-woogie pattern remains constant throughout. The right hand plays around with the melody of the song as in the figure below.

TRACK 24

*Figure 24 Melodic Comparison*

The right hand has particularly nice riffs at bars 15, 38–40, and 56–57.

TRACK 25

*Figure 25 – "Swanee River Boogie" in the style of Dr. John*

Dr. John's version of "Pine Top Boogie" is so unlike "Pine Top" Smith's original 1929 recording that it's like they are two completely different songs. However, Dr. John's version has a propulsive rhythm and is fun to play. It begins with a two-hand tremolo and double octaves in the melody, then briefly visits the main riff. At bar 17, a riff in 16th notes emphasizes sixths in the high register of the piano for a whole chorus.

At bar 29, the two-hand tremolo returns and a short theme in double octaves comes down the keyboard into another chorus. At bar 41, there's a new riff in sixths for a chorus. The two-hand tremolo returns for a restatement at bar 53 and the main riff finishes out the last chorus.

TRACK 26

*Figure 26 – "Pine Top Boogie Woogie" in the style of Dr. John*

**(The Original) Boogie Woogie**
By Clarence "Pine Top" Smith

Most boogie woogies are swing, but straight eighth-note boogie woogies are popular, too. Here's an excerpt from a straight-eighth boogie in the style of Professor Longhair called "Mess Around."

The basic left-hand pattern is a classic boogie-woogie pattern with walking octaves going up and then coming back down. "Mess Around" begins with two hands in double octaves playing the theme.

TRACK 27

*Figure 27 – "Mess Around" in the style of Professor Longhair*

**Mess Around**
Words and Music by Ahmet Ertegun
© 1954 (Renewed) UNICHAPPELL MUSIC INC.
All Rights Reserved   Used by Permission

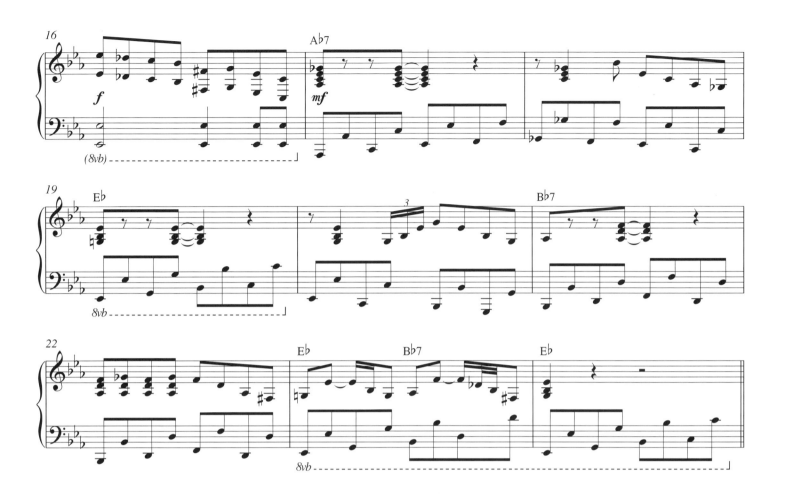

# CHAPTER 5
# R&B STYLES

In 1948, Jerry Wexler of *Billboard* magazine coined the term "rhythm and blues" as a musical marketing term, a catch-all reference to any music that was made by and for black Americans. It replaced the offensive term "race recordings." New Orleans piano players played a prominent role in the rhythm and blues of the late 1940s and early 1950s, which developed into rock 'n' roll.

**Antoine Dominique "Fats" Domino Jr.** was born in 1928 in New Orleans. He dropped out of school in the fourth grade to work in a factory. In 1949, he was playing blues and boogie hits of the day in local New Orleans clubs. His most popular song was "Swanee River Hop." Also popular was his raucous version of "The Junker's Blues," the tune that Champion Jack Dupree had recorded in 1940.

In 1949, Lew Chudd, the head of Imperial Records, was in New Orleans scouting new talent, when he decided to check out Fats Domino in the Ninth Ward. Along with local record producer Dave Bartholomew, he traveled to a ramshackle club where he was thrilled with Domino's version of "The Junker's Blues."

Chudd wasted no time. Approaching Domino, he pulled out his standard contract and asked, "How would you like to make records?" Domino signed Chudd's contract on the spot.

A few days later Fats was at Bartholomew's house, when Bartholomew told Fats that he was going to have to write new words to "The Junker's Blues." He suggested the title "The Fat Man." Domino and Bartholomew wrote the new words and a few days later the song was recorded.

The shuffle feel of "The Fat Man" is similar to the way Champion Jack Dupree played "The Junker's Blues," with heavy root and fifth action in both hands. This song, recorded on December 10, 1949, is considered by some to be the very first rock 'n' roll recording.

 *Figure 28 – Fats Domino blues intro*

Fats Domino became the biggest black rock 'n' roll star in the 1950s. He had more hits than any other '50s rocker besides Elvis Presley. He had 37 Top 40 singles. There were several stylistic modes that he used regularly in the piano parts of his singles.

By far, the most common of his styles was to use a strong triplet rhythm in the right hand of the piano in a fairly slow tempo. Here are two examples.

*Figure 29 – Triplet rhythm*

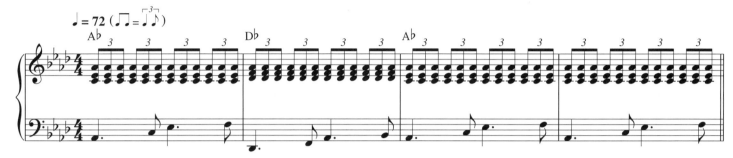

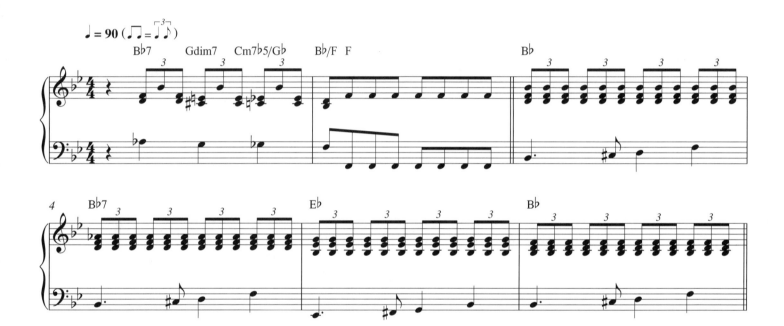

Also common was a two-hand shuffle rhythm in a fast tempo.

*Figure 30 – Fast Two-hand shuffle*

Some of Fats' hits featured a piano part that used a medium shuffle rhythm with a walking bass.

TRACK 31

*Figure 31 – Medium shuffle*

At times, Fats used a blues left-hand pattern.

TRACK 32

*Figure 32 – Blues left hand*

Occasionally he played a straight-eighth rhythm.

TRACK 33

*Figure 33 – Straight eighths*

Fats' best-remembered single, "Blueberry Hill," is a standard from the 1940s, but Domino treated the song as if it were a slow blues in 12/8. The left-hand pattern, based on broken chords, is the most common pattern in slow piano blues. The right hand plays triads in constant triplets.

TRACK 34

*Figure 34 – 12/8 slow blues pattern*

Domino's string of hits ended in the late 1960s with the British Invasion. His final hit was a 1968 cover of the Beatles' "Lady Madonna," which was ironic since Paul McCartney originally wrote the song in an emulation of Domino's piano style.

Another New Orleans legend of early rock 'n' roll was **Huey "Piano" Smith**, born in 1934. Smith's piano playing was influenced by boogie woogie styles, Jelly Roll Morton, Fats Domino, and Professor Longhair.

His biggest hits were "Rockin' Pneumonia and the Boogie Woogie Flu," "Don't You Just Know It," and "High Blood Pressure" in the years 1957–58. These novelty tunes were inspired by children's street poems and jump-rope rhythms.

Smith was best known for his shuffling right hand. Here's an example.

*Figure 35 – Huey Smith shuffle style*

TRACK 35

Sometimes Smith played "crushed" notes, i.e., major and minor thirds played at the same time.

**Figure 36 – Huey Smith crushed notes**

TRACK 36

Another technique he used frequently was tremolos.

*Figure 37 – Huey Smith tremolos*

TRACK 37

# CHAPTER 6
# PROFESSOR LONGHAIR'S STYLE

**Professor Longhair** (1918–1980) was born **Henry Roeland Byrd** and was also known as **Fess**.

Professor Longhair was the Godfather of New Orleans piano. His importance cannot be overemphasized. He was professionally active from 1948 to 1980. Virtually every New Orleans pianist to come after him has acknowledged his powerful influence. Allen Toussaint has called him "The Bach of Rock."

Fess taught himself how to play. He wasn't a technical virtuoso like James Booker, but he made up for that with rhythmic sophistication and originality.

He was a collector of rhythms. In the 1940s, he listened to and played with musicians from Cuba. He took the "Spanish Tinge," spoken of by Jelly Roll Morton, a kind of left-hand rhumba beat, and placed boogie-woogie and blues figures on top of it in the right hand. The result was a galloping hybrid dance music that was imbued with joy and spirit. His songs, like "Tipitina" and "Mardi Gras in New Orleans" are perennial classics.

He first recorded in 1949. He had one commercial hit, 1950s "Bald Head." He had a minor stroke in the 1950s and recuperated, coming back in 1957 with "No Buts No Maybes." In the 1960s, his career faltered and he became a janitor to support himself, but an appearance at the 1971 New Orleans Jazz & Heritage Festival restored his standing. He recorded his best album, *Crawfish Fiesta*, in 1979.

Professor Longhair recorded a number of tracks that didn't really fit into one of his regular styles, such as "Red Beans," "Crawfish Fiesta," and "Mess Around." But otherwise, Fess's musical output can basically be divided into three major styles.

First, there was the simple two-beat shuffle style he used on such tunes as "Bald Head," "Whole Lotta Lovin,'" and "No Buts No Maybes." This is a basic two-hand shuffle, not much different than Fats Domino's.

TRACK 38

*Figure 38 – Two-beat shuffle pattern*

Second, there was the standard 12/8 slow blues style of "Gone So Long," "Gonna Leave This Town," "Something on Your Mind," and "Mean Ol' World." There was some variety among his right-hand patterns, but all his 12/8 blues essentially used the 12/8 "Blueberry Hill" bass line.

*Figure 39 – 12/8 slow blues patterns*

Finally, there is his trademark, what became known as the "rhumba boogie." It's essentially the left-hand bass line in the figure below.

*Figure 40 – The rhumba boogie bass line*

The bass line has the same rhythm as the "Spanish Tinge" spoken of by Jelly Roll Morton. Sometimes this bass line was played in octaves. Fess had several variations for the right hand. Essentially the right hand played chords, but at times it was rhythmically active. Sometimes the rhumba boogie was played as a rhumba shuffle.

*Figure 41 – Two rhumba shuffle examples*

More often, it was played as a straight rhumba, with straight eighth notes.

*Figure 42 – Six straight rhumba examples*

All the rhumbas were based on 12-bar blues patterns. Fess would generally establish a two-handed accompaniment pattern and then just stick with it. On most songs, he simply played his two-handed accompaniment figure and sang, but occasionally he played piano solo. Following are some of his solo techniques.

Fess would play a sequence of notes then play it again, twice as fast. Note that he continued to play the rhumba boogie bass with his left hand.

*Figure 43 – Repeat twice as fast*

TRACK 43

He used thirds in his right hand.

TRACK 44

*Figure 44 – Thirds in right hand*

Occasionally, he would depart from his two-handed accompaniment pattern and play fills with his right hand. Note that the bass line is not a strict rhumba boogie.

TRACK 45

*Figure 45 – Fills with right hand*

He played tremolos that included blue notes.

TRACK 46

*Figure 46 – Tremolos with blue notes*

He would play a rhythm of four in the right hand against three in the left.

TRACK 47

*Figure 47 – Four against three*

He would play a rhythm of two in the right hand against three in the left.

TRACK 48

*Figure 48 – Two against three*

He would play a major seventh chord (instead of a dominant seventh chord) for the IV chord.

*Figure 49 – Major seventh IV chord*

TRACK 49

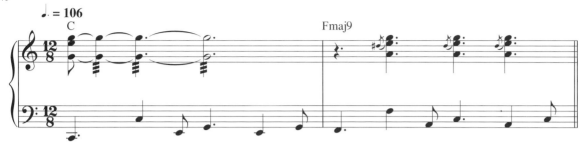

"Big Chief" is one of Professor Longhair's most popular songs. It's an infectious party song in straight eighth-note rhythm. This is an example of building a rollicking feel out of a minimum of musical materials – basically, broken chords emphasizing the alternation of the minor third (F♯) and the major third (G) of the E♭ tonic chord. The first part is a right-hand solo. The second part adds the rhumba bass. However, the bass line is not the typical broken-triad bass common to most of Professor Longhair's songs – it's a double-stop pattern instead.

*Figure 50 – "Big Chief"*

TRACK 50

# CHAPTER 7
# ALLEN TOUSSAINT'S STYLE

**Allen Toussaint** (*b*1938) is a great New Orleans pianist, but is probably better known as a songwriter, arranger, and record producer. He's worked with everyone from Glen Campbell to Bonnie Raitt to Ringo Starr to Christina Aguilera. His songs include "Working in the Coal Mine," "Southern Nights," and "Yes We Can Can." His piano has showed up on hundreds of records. He's had a hand in an astounding variety of chart records.

His chief piano influence was Professor Longhair.

He was inducted into the Rock and Roll Hall of Fame in 1998.

Toussaint included two traditional New Orleans compositions on his 2009 album, *The Bright Mississippi* – the traditional gospel song "Just a Closer Walk with Thee" and the folksong "St. James Infirmary." In "Just a Closer Walk with Thee," played with straight eighths, the solo clarinet plays the melody and Toussaint plays an insistent, bluesy accompaniment figure on the piano that lasts for the duration of the song. This figure seems to give impetus to the clarinetist, because he gives a beautiful performance.

Toussaint uses a lot of parallel tenth movement, particularly in bars 14–16 and bars 25–26. The arrangement has a real soulful feel.

*Figure 51 – "Just a Closer Walk with Thee"*

TRACK 51

**Just a Closer Walk with Thee**
Traditional
Copyright © 2013 by HAL LEONARD CORPORATION
International Copyright Secured  All Rights Reserved

In "St. James Infirmary" the piano plays the melody, right-hand only, for some 22 bars. There is effective use of blue notes in bars 15, 19, and 20. At bar 23, both hands play in unison, two octaves apart. At bar 32, the right hand plays in thirds with the left hand doubling the lower note an octave below. The piano part in this arrangement is fairly simple, but very striking.

TRACK 52

*Figure 52 – "St. James Infirmary"*

One can definitely hear echoes of Professor Longhair in Toussaint's playing. He wrote a wonderful tribute to Professor Longhair called "Tipitina and Me." Elvis Costello added lyrics and retitled it "Ascension Day" for the album *The River in Reverse*. We present the piano solo version here.

The song has a sweet, melancholy feel. It's a meditation on Professor Longhair's song "Tipitina," which is turned around and upside down and examined from different perspectives.

*Figure 53 – "Tipitina and Me"*

TRACK 53

# CHAPTER 8
# BALLAD STYLES

Not all New Orleans music is rocking party music. Ballads are an essential part of the music, too. Allen Toussaint has written many exquisite ballads. Here's a ballad in the style of his song "It's Raining." It's the essence of simplicity. Written in a flowing 6/8, the right hand basically plays triads on every principal beat while the left hand plays bass notes. The highlights are the B♭9 (♭VII) chord in bar 15, the D7♭5 chord in bar 21, the descending parallel tritones in bar 37, and the ending sequence starting at bar 43.

TRACK 54

*Figure 54 – In the style of "It's Raining" by Allen Toussaint*

Dr. John has a penchant for playing sentimental ballads that date from the early days of Tin Pan Alley. In this arrangement of "Cry Me a River," the melody is often played in octaves or chords that span an octave. The arrangement uses quite a bit of filigree (grace notes, tremolos, rolled chords, etc.) and the left hand is kept constantly moving.

*Figure 55 – "Cry Me a River" in the style of Dr. John*

TRACK 55

# CHAPTER 9
# OTHER PLAYERS AND THEIR STYLES

**Art Neville** (*b*1937) is a member of the Neville Brothers – along with his three brothers, Charles, Aaron, and Cyril. He also was a founding member of the Meters, a funk band based in New Orleans. The band was active from the late 1960s to 1977. With their funk anthems "Sophisticated Cissy" and "Cissy Strut," they are considered to be among the originators of funk music.

Neville played mostly Hammond B-3 organ in the Meters, but played some piano as well. Here are some funky piano vamps in the style of Art Neville.

TRACK 56

*Figure 56 – Art Neville funk riffs*

It wouldn't be right to mention funk without considering James Booker. Booker had an original funk style that involved playing a bass line in octaves with his left hand while his right hand played a complex pattern reminiscent of a Billy Preston clavinet riff. Here's an example.

*Figure 57 – James Booker funk riff*

TRACK 57

**Ellis Marsalis** (*b*1934) is the father of New Orleans modern jazz and the patriarch of the first family of jazz, the Marsalis family. Father of Wynton and Branford, he's made dozens of recordings and has made important contributions to jazz and musical education.

Here's a portion of his recorded version of "Do You Know What It Means to Miss New Orleans." Recorded with a trio, Marsalis uses the traditional style of three or four note rootless voicings in the left hand and the melody played in the right. He plays a two-hand voicing in bar 8; in bars 13–14, his left-hand voicings are particularly sparkling. It's a pleasing version of the song.

*Figure 58 – "Do You Know What It Means to Miss New Orleans"*

TRACK 58

**Do You Know What It Means to Miss New Orleans**
Written by Eddie De Lange and Louis Alter
© 1946 (Renewed 1974, 2002) DE LANGE MUSIC CO. and LOUIS ALTER MUSIC PUBLICATIONS, New York
All Rights for DE LANGE MUSIC CO. Administered by BUG MUSIC, INC., A BMG CHRYSALIS COMPANY
All Rights outside the United States Controlled by EDWIN H. MORRIS & COMPANY, A Division of MPL MUSIC PUBLISHING, INC.
All Rights Reserved   Used by Permission

64

**Henry Butler** (b1949) is an astonishing piano player with incredible technique. He performs and records volcanic, hypercharged versions of New Orleans blues and traditional jazz. He is also a speaker and educator in demand for conferences and college programs. Even though he's been blind since birth, Butler is an accomplished photographer. He spends most of his time in New York City.

Butler's version of "Basin Street Blues" is a kaleidoscope of styles. He incorporates many of the techniques we've studied thus far in a mere 24 bars. Note his use of walking-tenth triads in bar 2 and the tremolo in bar 3. Bars 5–6 are a traditional stride pattern, and he employs octave unisons in several places. We see tenth triads again in bars 10–11 and a boogie woogie-like bass line in bar 13. He applies a traditional blues left-hand figure in bars 18–19. Again, he utilizes walking tenth triads in bars 22–23 and, finally, a traditional turnaround in bar 24.

TRACK 59

## *Figure 59 – "Basin Street Blues"*

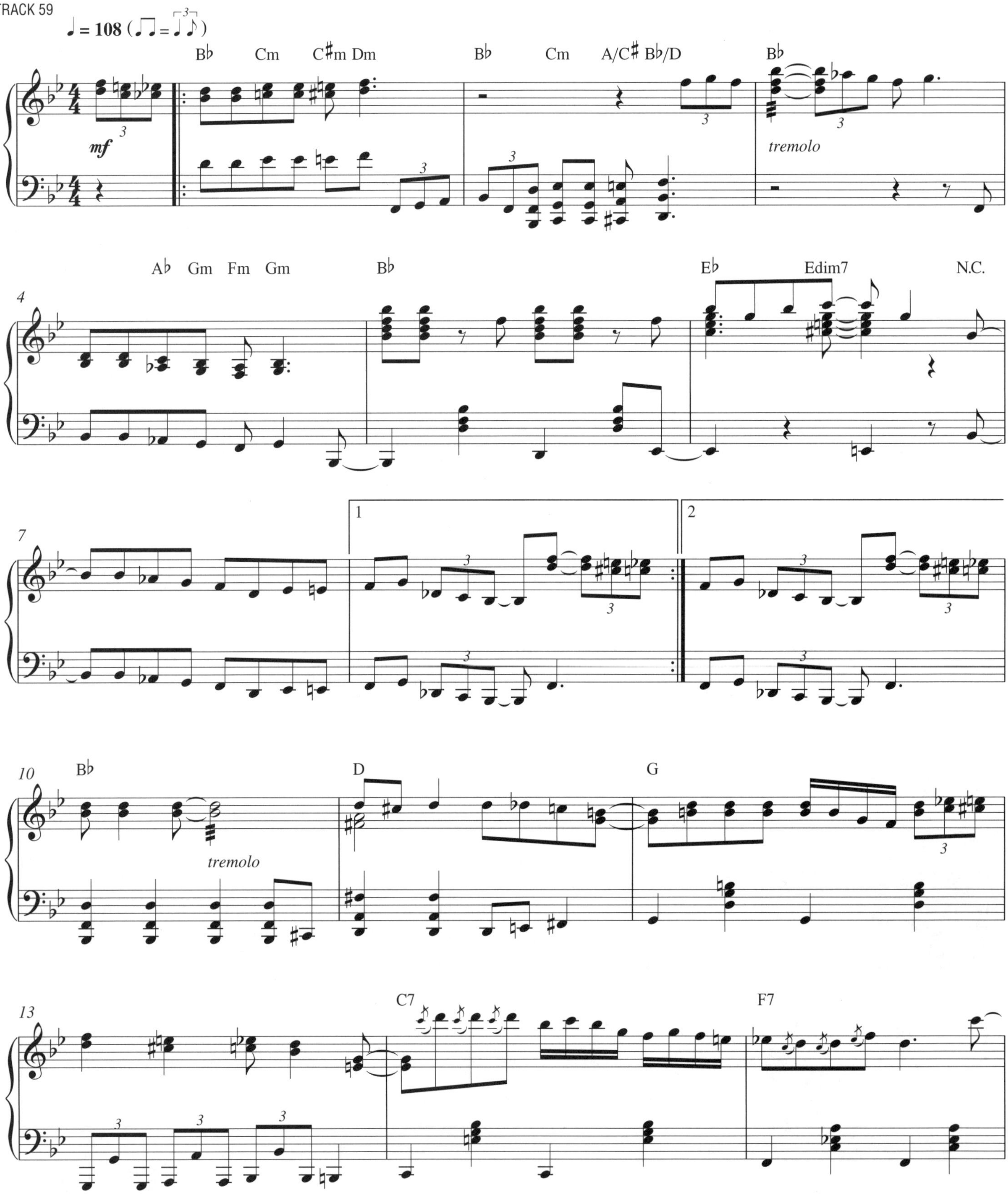

When one considers New Orleans piano players today, one doesn't necessarily think of **Harry Connick Jr.** (*b*1957). Connick is best known as a singer, bandleader, and actor. Enormously successful, he's sold over 25 million albums, has had seven Top 20 U.S. albums, has had ten No. 1 U.S. jazz albums, and has won three Grammy Awards.

But let's not forget that Connick first came to prominence as a pianist at a very young age. He was born and raised in New Orleans and he took lessons from both Ellis Marsalis and James Booker. Connick's first two albums, *Harry Connick, Jr.* (1987) and *20* (1988) are his best, showing off his New Orleans piano chops.

Let's see how student differs from teacher by looking at Connick's version of "On the Sunny Side of the Street." Unlike Booker, who used a chordal right hand throughout the piece, Connick plays the melody almost entirely in single note fashion. Also, unlike Booker, Connick plays the traditional stride pattern with his left hand – i.e., bass note, chord, bass note, chord. It's less complicated than Booker's arrangement, but it swings and it's a strong performance.

*Figure 60 "On the Sunny Side of the Street"*

**On the Sunny Side of the Street**
Lyric by Dorothy Fields
Music by Jimmy McHugh
Copyright © 1930 Shapiro, Bernstein & Co., Inc., New York and Cotton Club Publishing for the USA
Copyright Renewed
All Rights for Cotton Club Publishing Controlled and Administered by EMI April Music Inc.
International Copyright Secured   All Rights Reserved
Used by Permission

# CHAPTER 10
# DR. JOHN'S STYLE

**Malcolm John "Mac" Rebennack Jr.** (*b*1940) is better known by his stage name, Dr. John. He's a singer, songwriter, pianist, and guitarist whose music combines blues, pop, jazz, boogie woogie, and rock 'n' roll. He's the consummate New Orleans pianist and a tireless champion of Crescent City music.

When Rebennack was 13 years old, he met Professor Longhair and was deeply impressed. Active musically since the 1950s, Dr. John started out as a guitarist but switched to piano after his left ring finger was injured by a gunshot in a club fight. Professor Longhair was a major influence on his piano style.

Dr. John moved to Los Angeles in 1963, where he became a first-call session musician on the booming L.A. music scene. An addiction to heroin led to criminal activities and a series of arrests that ended in prison time. His sentence ended in 1965.

©Ray Avery/CTSIMAGES

He first came to prominence in the early 1970s with a wildly theatrical stage performance, inspired by medicine shows, Mardi Gras costumes, and voodoo ceremonies. He adopted the persona Dr. John the Night Tripper. In 1973, with Allen Toussaint producing and the Meters backing, Dr. John released the seminal New Orleans funk album, *In the Right Place*. Since the mid-1970s, Dr. John has focused on a blend of music that touches blues, New Orleans R&B, Tin Pan Alley standards, and more. He has made dozens of recordings, won five Grammy Awards, and was inducted into the Rock and Roll Hall of fame in 2011.

Dr. John might well be called the "Keeper of the Flame," as he has assumed the mantle of caretaker of his hometown's musical heritage. He is a veritable living archive of New Orleans piano music and lore. He's been featured in several video and audio New Orleans piano lessons published by Homespun Tapes. In addition to the instructional value, he provides historical context about many other blues artists.

For our next selection, we have version of "When the Saints Go Marching In" suitable for a New Orleans funeral. A traditional funeral in New Orleans begins with a march to the cemetery by the family, friends, and a brass band. The band plays slow, somber music. After the burial, though, the music cuts loose, representing a cutting loose of the spirit from the earthly tier. One could cut loose to this romp version of "Saints" in the style of Dr. John.

*Figure 61 – "When the Saints Go Marching In" romp style*

**When the Saints Go Marching In**
Words by Katherine E. Purvis
Music by James M. Black

# CHAPTER 11
# NEW ORLEANS PIANO TODAY

There's a younger generation following in the footsteps of those chronicled in this book.

**Jon Cleary** (*b*1962) is originally from Cranbrook in Kent, England. He moved to New Orleans at age 17. He's released seven CDs, including *Occapella*, a collection of Allen Toussaint songs. Cleary is steeped in the traditions of New Orleans R&B. At the drop of a hat, he can perform a Professor Longhair or James Booker number. In concert, Cleary performs the occasional cover ("Tipitina" or "Mardi Gras in New Orleans"), but his music leans heavily toward his original R&B and funk. He's performed with Bonnie Raitt and Dr. John, among others.

**Tom McDermott** (*b*1957) is a pianist and composer. Born in St. Louis, he moved to New Orleans and has become noted for the styles of jazz associated with that town. He's made 10 CDs as a leader and several as a sideman. He was in the Dukes of Dixieland for many years. He also co-founded and wrote arrangements for the New Orleans Nightcrawlers, an 11-piece brass band. McDermott puts his own spin on traditional jazz, reinventing works by Louis Moreau Gottschalk, Jelly Roll Morton, and Scott Joplin. He also records music of Brazil as well as his own compositions. He, too, is intimately familiar with the music of Professor Longhair and James Booker.

**Joe Krown** plays jazzy and funky Hammond B-3 organ with his band, the Joe Krown Organ Combo. But he also plays piano in the traditional New Orleans style and has recorded several albums.

**Davell Crawford** (*b*1975) is a singer and keyboardist. Born into a musical family, he has been performing since the age of seven. He plays piano and B-3 organ and has deep gospel roots.

**David Torkanowsky** has recorded a CD entitled *Steppin' Out*. Torkanowsky is a mainstream jazz player whose best-known recording is a version of "Spring Can Really Hang You Up the Most."

**Joshua Paxton** has a CD called *Alone at Last* (2009). It's mostly standards and includes a Booker-inspired version of Prince's "Kiss." Paxton has transcribed two folios of New Orleans piano music, published by Hal Leonard Corporation.

These are just a few of the younger generation. In years to come, new generations will no doubt extend the city's musical language.

# MATERIALS FOR FURTHER STUDY

## INTERESTING READING

*Blue Monday: Fats Domino and the Lost Dawn of Rock 'n' Roll*
    by Rick Coleman, Da Capo Press (2007)
    ISBN: 978-0306815317

*I Hear You Knockin': The Sound of New Orleans Rhythm and Blues*
    by Jeff Hannusch, Swallow Publications (1985)
    ISBN: 978-0961424503

*Musical Gumbo: The Music of New Orleans*
    by Grace Lichtenstein and Laura Dankner, W.W. Norton & Co. (1993)
    ISBN: 978-0393034684

*Under a Hoodoo Moon: The Life of the Night Tripper*
    by Dr. John (Mac Rebennack) and Jack Rummel, St. Martin's Griffin (1995)
    ISBN: 978-0312131975

*Up from the Cradle of Jazz: New Orleans Music Since World War II*
    by Jason Berry, Jonathan Foose, and Tad Jones, University of Louisiana at Lafayette Press (2009)
    ISBN: 978-1887366878

## ESSENTIAL LISTENING

James Booker
    *Junco Partner*, Hannibal (1993)
    *New Orleans Piano Wizard: Live!*, Rounder Records (1992)

Henry Butler
    *Blues and More*, Windham Hill (1992)
    *For All Seasons*, Atlantic Records (1996)

Harry Connick Jr.
    *Harry Connick Jr.*, Columbia Records (1987)
    *20*, Columbia Records (1988)

Fats Domino
    *Greatest Hits: Walking to New Orleans*, Capitol Records (2007)

Dr. John
    *Dr. John Plays Mac Rebennack*, Clean Cuts (2002)
    *Dr. John's Gumbo*, Electra/WEA (1990)
    *Goin' Back to New Orleans*, Warner Bros. (1992)

Champion Jack Dupree
    *Blues from the Gutter*, Atlantic Jazz (2011)

Professor Longhair
    *Mardi Gras in New Orleans*, Night Hawk Records (1990)
    *Crawfish Fiesta*, Alligator Records, 1990

Huey "Piano" Smith
*The Best of Huey "Piano" Smith*, Fuel (2000, 2009)

Allen Toussaint
*The Bright Mississippi*, Nonesuch (2009)
*The River in Reverse* (with Elvis Costello), Verve Forecast (2006)

Tuts Washington
*New Orleans Piano Professor*, Rounder (2009)

# RECORDINGS BY TODAY'S ARTISTS

Jon Cleary
*Alligator Lips and Dirty Rice*, Megaforce (2006)
*Do Not Disturb*, FHQ Records (2006)
*Jon Cleary and the Absolute Monster Gentlemen*, Basin Street Records (2002)
*Mo Hippa*, MRI Associated (2008)
*Moonburn*, Pointblank (2000)
*Occapella*, FHQ Records (2012)
*Pin Your Spin*, Basin Street Records (2004)

Davell Crawford
*Born With the Funk*, Mardi Gras Records (1999)
*Let Them Talk*, Rounder (2009)
*Love Like Yours and Mine*, Bullseye Records (1999)
*The B-3 and Me*, Bullseye Records (1998)

Joe Krown
*Buckle Up*, STR Digital (2000)
*Down and Dirty*, STR Digital (1999)
*Exposed*, CD Baby (2012)
*Funk Yard*, STR Digital (2002)
*Just the Piano, Just the Blues*, STR Digital (1998)
*Live at Jazz Fest*, Munck Music (2011)
*Live at the Maple Leaf*, Independent (2011)
*Livin' Large*, Independent (2005)
*Old Friends*, Independent (2011)
*New Orleans Piano Rolls*, STR Digital (2003)

Tom McDermott
*All the Keys and Then Some*, Parnassus (2008)
*Almost Native* (with Evan Christopher), Threadhead Records (2011)
*Bamboula*, Bananastan LLC (2012)
*Choro do Norte*, STR Digital (2005)
*Creole Nocturne*, Arbors Records (2008)
*Danza*, STR Digital (2002)
*Live at Chickie Wah Wah* (with Meschiya Lake), CDBY (2012)
*Live in Paris*, STR Digital (2007)
*New Orleans Duets*, CD Baby (2008)
*The Crave*, STR Digital (2001)

Joshua Paxton
*Alone at Last*, Joshua Paxton (2009)

David Torkanowsky
*Steppin' Out*, Rounder Select (1992)

# DVDS

*Dr. John Teaches New Orleans Piano*, 2 DVDs with written materials
DVD 1: Hal Leonard (HL00641839)
DVD 2: Hal Leonard (HL00641840)

*The Piano Styles of Dr. John*, 2 DVDs with written materials
Hal Leonard (HL00641617)

# BOOK/CD PACKAGES

*Dr. John Teaches New Orleans Piano, Vol. 1*
Hal Leonard (HL00699090)

*Dr. John Teaches New Orleans Piano, Vol. 2*
Hal Leonard (HL00699093)

*Dr. John Teaches New Orleans Piano, Vol. 3*
Hal Leonard (HL00699094)

*Dr. John Teaches New Orleans and the Roots of Rock* (book with 4 CDs)
Hal Leonard (HL00641692)

*Best of Blues Piano* by Todd Lowry
Hal Leonard (HL00695841)

# SHEET MUSIC FOLIOS

*New Orleans Piano Legends*, 11 Transcriptions
Hal Leonard (HL00310092)

*The James Booker Collection*, 10 Transcriptions
Hal Leonard (HL00306224)

*Professor Longhair Collection*, 19 Transcriptions
Hal Leonard (HL00306221)

*Elvis Costello and Allen Toussaint: The River in Reverse*
Hal Leonard (HL00306839)

# INDEX OF PIANISTS